After the law had been passed, Senator Mark Hatfield spoke to the Roseburg, Oregon students who had contributed so much to the drive to save the mustangs.

"This is a real victory for you," he told the gathered students and teachers. He went on to praise the students for their willingness to take an active part in the government of their country. "Even though you can't vote yet, you have the right to make recommendations to the government," he pointed out. . . .

SAVE THE MUSTANGS!
was originally published
by Julian Messner.

Critics' Corner:

"An interesting and lively case study of how private citizens can influence the government to create new laws. . . . Following each phase of the legislative process, Weiss clearly puts a great deal of information about wild horses and lawmaking into her crisp account." —*School Library Journal*

Also recommended by: A.L.A. Booklist. Winner of the Christopher Award, 1974.

About the Author:

ANN E. WEISS was born in Newton, Massachusetts and attended public schools in nearby Rockland. She graduated from Brown University in 1965. For seven years she was an associate editor at Scholastic Magazines, Inc. She worked on two publications for fourth graders. Ms. Weiss now lives in Whitefield, Maine, where she and her husband write books and articles for young readers. They also enjoy gardening and restoring their 160-year-old farmhouse.

SAVE THE
MUSTANGS!

SAVE THE MUSTANGS!

(Original title: Save the Mustangs!
How a Federal Law Is Passed)

BY ANN E. WEISS
Illustrated with photographs

AN ARCHWAY PAPERBACK
POCKET BOOKS • NEW YORK

SAVE THE MUSTANGS!

Julian Messner edition published 1974

Archway Paperback edition published September, 1976

PHOTO CREDITS

Baltimore Sun: pp. 16-17
Bureau of Land Management: Title page, p. 5, pp. 20-21
William Grigg: p. 35
Mary Lea: p. 42, p. 51, pp. 52-53
Ira Mandelbaum-Scope: p. 18, p. 24, p. 33, p. 58, p. 70, p. 72
The News-Review, Roseburg, Oregon: p. 10, p. 38, p. 82
Pleasant Valley School, Fairmont, West Virginia: p. 12, p. 31
Dr. Roger L. Slocum: p. 3, p. 62
United Press International Photos: pp. 26-27, p. 45, pp. 80-81
Wide World Photos: p. xiv, pp. 48-49, p. 55, p. 65, p. 86
Wild Horse Organized Assistance: p. 14

Published by
POCKET BOOKS, a division of Simon & Schuster, Inc.,
A GULF+WESTERN COMPANY
630 Fifth Avenue, New York, N.Y. 10020.

Archway Paperback editions are distributed in the U.S. by Simon & Schuster, Inc., 630 Fifth Avenue, New York, N.Y. 10020, and in Canada by Simon & Schuster of Canada, Ltd., Markham, Ontario, Canada.

ISBN: 0-671-29786-4.
Library of Congress Catalog Card Number: 73-18355.
This Archway Paperback edition is published by arrangement with Julian Messner. Copyright, ©, 1974, by Ann E. Weiss. All rights reserved. *Save the Mustangs!* was originally published under the title *Save the Mustangs! How a Federal Law Is Passed*. This book, or portions thereof, may not be reproduced by any means without permission of the original publisher: Julian Messner, a division of Simon & Schuster, Inc., 1 West 39th Street, New York, New York 10018.
Printed in the U.S.A.

Acknowledgments

The author gratefully acknowledges the help of the following people, whose kind assistance made possible detailed reconstruction of many of the events leading to the final passage of P.L. 92-195: Senators Mark Hatfield, Oregon, and Henry Jackson, Washington; Representatives Walter Baring, Nevada, John Dellenback, Oregon, and Gilbert Gude, Maryland; Mrs. William L. Blue, American Horse Protection Association; Joan Bolsinger, Roseburg, Oregon; Velma Johnston, Reno, Nevada; and Dr. Anne V. Young, Principal, Brookville School, Glen Head, New York.

For
Margot Elizabeth Weiss

Contents

CHAPTER

1
"There Ought to Be a Law" *1*

2
The War of the Pencils *7*

3
Birth of a Bill *19*

4
Speaking Up for Mustangs *37*

5
Two Acts Equal—No Law *59*

6
A Law at Last *73*

7
Making It Work *87*

Glossary *91*

Index *95*

SAVE THE
MUSTANGS!

Panic-stricken mustangs race across the barren flatland, herded by a "flying cowhand" in a noisy plane. On the ground, other mustangers pepper the wild horses with buckshot. Wounded and terrified, the animals will be driven into a hidden corral. This is just one cruel method of mustanging that was common in 1970.

1
"There Ought to Be a Law"

Heads high, tails streaming, a band of mustangs dashes madly down a steep mountain slope. Overhead, a small plane circles low, diving at the horses. From the plane's wing tip, a shrieking siren dangles.

A blast of buckshot bursts from the plane. The bullets strike the eyes, necks, and bodies of the wildly running animals. The smallest colt falters, and falls far behind the others. Left without his mother, he will starve to death.

The other mustangs are off the mountain now, rushing pell-mell over the flatland. Again, the plane swoops low; again, buckshot spurts from its window. Panic-stricken, the horses stampede into a cleverly hidden corral.

Now the hunters—mustangers—rope the wounded animals and drag them to a waiting truck. Here the horses are crowded aboard, and a 300-mile trip begins.

During this trip, the horses are neither fed nor watered. Crazed by their suffering, they bite and kick one another. Blood seeps through the truck's floor, and drips onto the road.

Hours later, the truck reaches its destination: a slaughterhouse. There the mustangers sell their cargo for six cents a pound.

The mustangs, so lately running wild and free, will be made into pet food.

Horrified, a fourth-grade class in Roseburg, Oregon, listened to their teacher describe this brutal scene.

"Does that really happen, Miss Bolsinger?" one girl wanted to know.

Joan Bolsinger nodded. "Look, I was reading about it last night." She held up a book. "Let me tell you about the 'wild ones.'"

Eagerly, the boys and girls leaned forward. They loved stories about horses.

"Horses haven't always lived in America," Miss Bolsinger began. "The first Spanish explorers had to bring their own horses to the New World. Some of these horses escaped. Their descendants are the mustangs of today.

Corralled now, the mustangs suffer from hunger, thirst, exhaustion, and gunshot wounds. But the mustangers who captured the "wild ones" will show no mercy. The horses will be forced into a truck, carted off to a slaughterhouse, sold, and made into pet food.

SAVE THE MUSTANGS!

Some people believe the word 'mustang' comes from the Spanish word *mestengo,* which means 'without master or owner; wild.'"

"Do mustangs look like other horses?"

Miss Bolsinger looked up from her book.

"The wild ones are smaller than most horses you've probably seen," she replied. "But they are extremely tough. They have to be, living in the high mountains and narrow canyons where they hide from man. Some people say the wild ones are ugly. If you look at pictures of them, you'll agree with me—the mustangs are beautiful, running free across the open range."

"I bet mustangs helped carry mail on the Pony Express," a student suggested.

"That's right." Miss Bolsinger smiled. "They pulled pioneers' wagons, too. They carried supplies for the Lewis and Clark Expedition right here to Oregon. The Indians valued them highly."

"The mustangs are part of American history, all right," a girl said.

"How many are left now?" someone else asked.

"In 1900, there were about two million," said the teacher. "But now, in 1970, only 17,000—maybe only 10,000—remain. They live in a few Western states. Men have hunted

The freedom and beauty of the mustangs captured the imaginations of a few Americans like the fourth graders of Roseburg, Oregon. They told others of the need to protect these dying symbols of the Old West before it was too late.

and killed them for sport. Some ranchers shoot horses so their sheep and cattle can eat grass the mustangs might use. And they are sold for pet food. Soon there may be no mustangs left."

Suddenly, Miss Bolsinger stopped. It was clear that her students were very angry.

"There ought to be a law against hurting the wild ones," one student called out.

"There ought to be a law." With these words, the Roseburg fourth graders began a year of hard and exciting work. They waged a "pencil war," sending letters to Congressmen asking for a law to protect the horses. They wrote to schools all over the country to win support for their cause. One boy in the class even traveled three thousand miles to Washington, D.C., to tell lawmakers why the horses should be saved.

During the year, the fourth graders found out a lot about how our government works. They learned that people can make laws. They found out that, as American citizens, they themselves could help an idea become a law.

That's what this book is about.

2
The War of the Pencils

Joan Bolsinger and her students lost no time in beginning to fight for the mustang protection law they wanted.

The fourth graders' first step was to learn just how our laws are made—and by whom.

From textbooks and encyclopedias, the class found out that the chief United States lawmaking body is Congress, which meets in Washington, D.C., the nation's capital. There, Congressmen and Congresswomen discuss *bills*. A bill is a proposed law, set down in writing. Any member of Congress may introduce a bill, but not all bills finally become law.

Of course, Congress is not our only lawmaking body. Towns and cities also have lawmakers who pass laws to protect their citizens. A town law might be that all dogs must be kept on leashes, or that cars can go 25 miles an hour on the main street. State lawmakers pass laws, too. A state law might say that all people working in the state must be paid at least a certain amount of money per hour. Other state laws deal with safety standards, road building and repair, businesses carried on within the state, taxes, and so forth.

Laws of each city and state affect only the people who live, work, visit, or do business there. Congress alone has the power to make laws for the entire country.

Miss Bolsinger's students also learned that Congress is divided into two parts: the Senate and the House of Representatives. The Senate has one hundred members—two from each state. Senators are elected for six-year terms of office.

Members of the House of Representatives are elected to two-year terms. (Of course, Representatives, like Senators, may be re-elected over and over.) The House has 435 members, making it much larger than the Senate. But membership in the House is not evenly divided among the states.

Instead, membership in the House of Representatives is based on population. The more

The War of the Pencils

people living in a state, the more Representatives that state sends to Congress.

There is another difference between the House and the Senate. A state's Senators are elected by voters from all parts of the state. But each Representative is chosen by people in a single area, or *district,* of the state.

Armed with these facts, Miss Bolsinger's students decided that writing to Oregon's Congressmen would be their first step in working for a save-the-horses law.

Miss Bolsinger added another suggestion: writing to students in other schools to tell them about the mustangs. "Then these boys and girls can write to their Congressmen, too," she pointed out. "Senators and Representatives won't pass a law unless they know that many people want it. We'll need lots of people writing letters."

"Let's have a pencil war!" Waving his pencil, a boy leaped to his feet.

And so the "pencil war" began. A reporter on the Roseburg newspaper heard the phrase and wrote a story about the fourth graders' efforts. The idea spread.

In Eugene, Oregon, a junior high school class read about the pencil war and decided to send letters to Oregon Senator Mark Hat-

"Let's have a pencil war!" cried a Roseburg fourth grader. His pencil, waving in the air, became a symbol of the fight by American boys and girls to get Congress to pass a law to end mustanging forever.

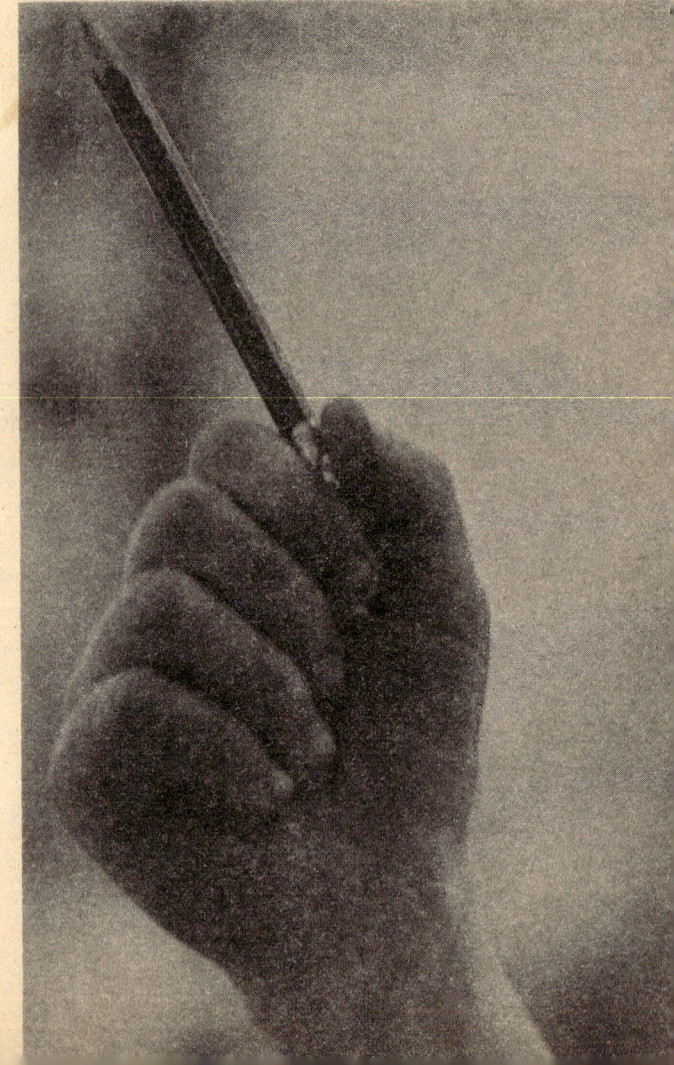

The War of the Pencils

field telling him about their concern for the mustangs. One boy wrote:

The Honorable Mark Hatfield
United States Senate,
Washington, D.C.
Dear Mr. Hatfield:
    I think the Wild Mustangs are part of our American heritage. They should be put on a special game reserve, safe from the dog food manufacturers. I'm sure that they can find another source of horse meat. But why drive the Mustangs into extinction?

                  Sincerely yours,
                  Steve McCune

In only a few weeks, the pencil war had reached far beyond Oregon. People around the country were writing to ask their Congressmen to support a wild-horse protection law.

Efforts to save the horses were coming from other sources, as well. In December, 1970, the same month that Miss Bolsinger and her students learned about the mustangs, students around the country read about the horses in a magazine used in many schools. The next month, an article about the horses

SAVE THE MUSTANGS!

Across the country, students joined the campaign to save the remaining wild horses. A class in Fairmont, West Virginia, whipped up local interest in the project by setting up a display about the mustangs' past, present, and future. Included in the display: posters, books about mustangs, scenes of the long-ago West.

appeared in *National Geographic* magazine. Children and grownups alike were fascinated by the magazine's colorful photos of the free-running mustangs. And they shuddered at the description of man's brutality toward the animals. Many of these people, too, began demanding a law to protect the "wild ones."

It was now January—time for a new session of Congress to begin. By law, Congress meets each January. Every odd-numbered year—1971, 1973, 1975—a "new" Congress opens. That is because elections to Congress

The War of the Pencils

are held the November of each even-numbered year—1970, 1972, 1974.

In January, 1971, the first session of the Ninety-Second Congress opened. In 1972, the second session of the Ninety-Second Congress began, and in 1973, the first session of the Ninety-Third Congress.

The opening date of the first session of the Ninety-Second Congress was set for Monday, January 21. In Bethesda, Maryland, an 11-year-old boy was determined to get a save-the horses bill introduced on the very day Congress opened. The boy was Gregory Gude, son of Maryland Representative Gilbert Gude.

For Christmas, Greg had received a book about the efforts of a Reno, Nevada, woman to save the mustangs. Velma Johnston had watched the "wild ones" as she grew up in the Nevada countryside. One day, after seeing a truckload of wounded and dying horses being hauled to a slaughterhouse, she started her fight to end mustanging.

In 1959, Mrs. Johnston—nicknamed Wild Horse Annie—helped get Congress to pass a law against the use of airplanes to hunt wild horses. From his other reading, though, Greg knew that mustangers had found ways to get around the Wild Horse Annie Law.

Of all those who worked to save the mustangs, perhaps the most dedicated has been Velma Johnston, nicknamed Wild Horse Annie. In 1959, she helped get Congress to pass a mustang protection law, but that law was not strong enough. So, she set to work again, writing to Congressmen, speaking to horse-protection societies, writing a newsletter to inform Americans about the plight of the wild ones.

The War of the Pencils

The law's loophole was that it *did* allow ranchers to use planes to round up their own runaway domestic horses. So mustangers would let domestic horses mingle with the wild herds. Then they would round up *all* the horses—using planes—and claim they only meant to capture the domestics. The mustangs, they would say, had been caught by accident. Of course, by the time the mustangers confessed to the "accident," the captured mustangs had already been sold and slaughtered.

Greg Gude told his father the facts. "We need a law that will really protect the horses," he added.

"Should Congress worry about horses that live in only a few states?" Mr. Gude asked. "I represent the people of a small part of Maryland. Probably no one in my district has ever even seen a mustang. My job is to work for laws that will help the men and women in my district."

"The wild ones are important to all Americans," Greg argued. "They're part of our history."

"Well, Greg, I'll look into it," Mr. Gude promised.

For days, Greg kept after his father about

the horses. "He was quite a lobbyist," joked Mr. Gude.

Real lobbyists are men and women who are paid to work for organizations such as businesses, veterans' groups, and conservation societies. They urge Congressmen to vote for bills that will favor the organization they represent. Most lobbyists work in Washington, but Greg did his "lobbying" over the Gude dinner table!

He wondered: Would his lobby succeed?

Capitol's Youngest Lobbyis[t]

By JOHN B. O'DONNELL, JR.
Washington Bureau of The Sun

Washington, April 20—Greg Gude, the 11-year-old son of Maryland's Eighth district congressman, lost his unofficial title of youngest lobbyist on Capitol Hill today to a 10-year-old Orego[nian]

Hatfield (R., Ore.), Lynn read [a] brief, prepared statement u[rg]ing adoption of the legislati[on] and his efforts to get the Oreg[on] legislature to recognize the a[ni]mals' plight.

The long parade of witness[es] also included Mrs. Velma Johnston, of R[eno,] 20-year

In the spring of 1971, headlines like this one appeared in newspapers. Reporters wrote story after story about the efforts of Americans—including hundreds of thousands of grade schoolers—to convince Congress that it should pass a wild horse protection bill.

Testify For Wild Horse Bill

stern ranges, but they have but disappeared.

Boyd L. Rasmussen, director the Interior Department's Bureau of Land Management, tested today that there are at sent 9,500 unclaimed, free-ming horses and about 10,000 claimed free-roaming burros.

Unprotected by law ses have been hun d, either fo

ago of legislation to prohibit the use of airplanes and mechanized vehicles for capturing and killing the horses on public lands.

But, she lamented, the legislation has not been effective, and efforts on the state level to provide protection for the horses "have failed miserably."

hile calling n to

A Congressman's (or Congresswoman's) office is a busy place. There, the Congressman's staff—the people working for him—help him sort through and answer mail, decide what bills to introduce, and help him keep in touch with the people "back home" who elected him.

3
Birth of a Bill

Greg's plea that his father introduce a bill in the House of Representatives was only one such request that the Congressman received in January, 1971. Hundreds of his other constituents, the people living in his district, had ideas for new laws, too. Laws to improve health care, to lower taxes, to pay for more schools, to send less money to needy nations—these are just a few of the suggestions that any Congressman receives daily.

Each Congressman has a staff that goes through his mail. Together, the Congressman and the people working for him decide which requests are most important, and exactly which bills he should introduce to Congress.

Congressman Gude asked one of his staff

While children and adults lobbied on behalf of the horses, and while Congressmen wondered whether to introduce or support wild horse protection bills, the mustang population continued to dwindle. At the turn of the century, there had been about two million

wild ones. By 1970, only a few thousand remained. Even those which lived on United States government lands might be rounded up and killed if government agents decided their numbers were growing too fast.

members to look into the wild horse situation. "Will the mustangs really die out unless they are protected?" he wanted to know. "Greg seems to think they will. Why aren't they already protected just the way other wildlife is? And find out whether it's really up to Congress—rather than to the states—to pass a save-the-horses law."

Within a few days, the Congressman received a report from his staff. The report backed up Greg's warning that without protection the mustangs would soon die out. It pointed out that wild burros were also in danger of extinction. According to the report, neither the horses nor the burros were protected because both were classed as feral (domestic animals gone wild) rather than as wildlife.

Finally, the report stated that many wild horses and burros range on public lands. These lands belong to the government of the United States and, therefore, to all the people of the United States.

Congressman Gude sat back and thought. Clearly, the horses needed protection. Since they roamed over land that belonged to all Americans, the horses were Maryland's concern as much as Nevada's or Oregon's.

Mr. Gude made up his mind. He *would*

Birth of a Bill

sponsor a save-the-horses bill. First the bill would have to be written, and for that, he turned to a lawyer.

The Congressman explained the type of bill he wanted. It would have to outlaw selling the mustangs—dead or alive. It would have to provide for setting up ranges where the horses could be protected. The penalty for breaking the law would be one year in prison or a $1,000 fine—or both.

The lawyer's first step was to look up present laws about mustangs and about the use of public lands. He had to make sure no other national laws conflicted with the bill Mr. Gude wanted written. Suppose a law said that animal ranges could not be established on public lands. Then the lawyer would have to write into Mr. Gude's bill a section repealing (taking back) that law.

The lawyer did not find any such conflicting laws. However, he did read the Wild Horse Annie Law and he spotted the loophole that allowed mustangers to continue their slaughter by mixing their own horses with the "wild ones." "We'll try not to leave *any* loopholes this time," he thought as he began to write the bill.

Sure enough, when Mr. Gude read the finished bill, he was pleased to see a section that

A Congressman at work in his Washington, D.C., office. Constituents' letters, newspaper articles, and staff reports cover his desk. The phone is kept busy with incoming and outgoing calls. Also on hand is a TV for up-to-the-minute news reports.

Birth of a Bill

outlawed releasing domestic horses into wild bands. He also noticed that the lawyer defined the animals to be protected as "all unbranded horses and burros on public lands."

"Now it won't matter that the mustangs are classified as feral," he said to himself. "Even though they are domestic animals gone wild, they will be protected anyway."

The Congressman had many other bills, reports, and letters waiting to be read, so he quickly looked over the rest of the bill. Section Three provided for setting up special mustang ranges. It also forbade selling any part of a mustang or burro.

Another section outlined penalties for breaking the law. The last section provided for money to allow the government to set up and manage the ranges.

Satisfied, Mr. Gude set the bill down on his desk and turned to other work.

That night at dinner, he announced the news to his son. "I'm introducing that save-the-horses bill after all, Greg." Then he added, "Would you like to come to the House and see me do it?"

"You bet!" Greg grinned happily.

On Monday, January 21, Greg Gude walked into the House of Representatives and took a seat.

On Monday, January 21, 1971, Greg Gude attended the opening day of the Ninety-Second Congress. As a visitor, Greg sat in the gallery on the upper level. His father, Maryland Representative Gilbert Gude, sat with the other Congressmen and Congresswomen on the lower level. The Speaker of the House is directly in front of the United States flag.

SAVE THE MUSTANGS!

Eagerly, Greg stared around. House members were moving about, greeting old friends as well as new Representatives. Bits of news were exchanged, and Representatives chatted about the bills they were planning to introduce. Greg hoped his father was getting in a good word for the mustangs.

Up front, Greg could see the Speaker of the House. The Speaker, elected by his fellow Representatives, runs the meetings of the House. He calls each meeting to order, and recognizes (calls on) Representatives who wish to speak.

In the Senate, meetings are run by the Vice President of the country. It is his job to act as President of the Senate. Since the Vice President has many duties besides that of running the Senate, the Senate elects a "temporary president" to run meetings at which the Vice President cannot be present.

Suddenly, Greg was startled out of his thoughts. His father was walking toward the Speaker. On the Speaker's desk rested a large basket—the hopper. Greg saw his father drop the save-the-horses bill into the hopper. The bill had been officially introduced!

Once, bills introduced in the House were read aloud to the members. This was called the *First Reading*. But because there are so

Birth of a Bill

many bills introduced now, that is no longer possible. On this opening day of Congress alone, 2,142 bills were placed in the hopper. No one would have time to read them all aloud. Today, the *First Reading* simply means that the Bill Clerk gives each bill a number. (The Bill Clerk is not a Representative. He is one of the many people who work for the House of Representatives.) The Bill Clerk numbered the Gude bill H.R. 795, showing that it was the 795th bill introduced in this session of the House of Representatives.

The same night, H.R. 795 went to the Government Printing Office. Next morning, every Senator and Representative had a printed copy of the bill to read and study.

Bills may be introduced in the Senate, too, although not all House bills are matched by a Senate version. In this case, though, several Senators were already busy working out save-the-horses bills. Two of these Senators, Mark Hatfield of Oregon and Henry Jackson of Washington, decided to sponsor a bill together.

Why? Senator Hatfield was a Republican and Senator Jackson a Democrat. The Republicans and the Democrats are this country's two major political parties. Nearly all members of Congress belong to either one of these parties.

Often, Democrats and Republicans oppose each other in Congress. Usually they have different ideas on our country's policies. If most Democrats vote for a particular bill, most Republicans will probably vote against it.

However, votes in Congress are not always divided according to party. Sometimes, a Congressman strongly favors a bill that other members of his own party oppose. He may vote for the bill in spite of his party. Or a Congressman may vote for or against a bill according to the kind of people he represents. Suppose Congress is considering a bill that would raise the prices farmers can get for their crops. Congressmen—Republican and Democratic—from farming states will probably vote *for* the bill. Republicans and Democrats from nonfarming states may vote *against* it.

Sometimes Congressmen think a bill is important to all Americans—no matter what their political party or where they live. Senators Hatfield and Jackson believed theirs was such a bill. By cosponsoring the save-the-horses bill, they hoped to get both Republicans and Democrats to vote for it.

On March 4, 1971, Senator Jackson introduced the bill in the Senate. Introduction of a

Members of a sixth-grade class display letters from their Congressmen. The boys and girls had urged the law-makers to work for a strong save-the-horses law. The Congressmen thanked the students for their letters and promised to vote for such a bill.

SAVE THE MUSTANGS!

bill there is more formal than it is in the House.

The President of the Senate recognized Senator Jackson. The Senator rose.

"Mr. President," he said, "on behalf of the Senior Senator from Oregon [Mr. Hatfield] and myself, I introduce today a bill designed to protect the last of the wild horses and burros of the United States—the living symbols of our historic pioneer spirit and the nobility of freedom. . . . Hundreds of school children throughout the country . . . plead for and demand federal protection for all existing bands of wild horses and burros. . . ."

The Hatfield-Jackson bill, too, was assigned a number—S. 1116. This bill and Congressman Gude's were not the only save-the-horses bills introduced in the Ninety-Second Congress. In all, four such bills were introduced in the Senate and 16 in the House. Already, the pencil wars—not just in Roseburg, but across the country—were raising lawmakers' interest in mustangs!

Now supporters of the save-the-horses bills faced a problem. How could they get Congress to consider these particular bills out of all the thousands of other bills that had been introduced? Congress does not have time to discuss and vote on all bills that are introduced. Just

Sometimes, citizens send a petition—a formal written request for a particular action—to their Congressmen. Here, a group of young women present a petition to their Senator. In the background is the dome of the United States Capitol, where Congress meets.

SAVE THE MUSTANGS!

the year before, a save-the-horses bill had been introduced and completely ignored.

"How can we keep that from happening again?" Greg Gude asked his father.

"Publicity will help," the Congressman replied.

A newspaper reporter on the Washington *Star* wrote about Greg's efforts to save the horses. Within days, Greg was receiving hundreds of letters, many of them from girls and boys. He couldn't answer them all, so he and his father mailed printed petitions that the horses be protected. The youngsters signed these petitions and mailed them to their own Senators and Representatives.

"These petitions convinced a lot of Congressmen and women to join as sponsors of the bill," Mr. Gude said later.

Other people helped. A group called the American Horse Protection Association held an exhibit of drawings and paintings of horses in Washington. One day, a horse and pony trotted down the busy street where the display was being held. Greg rode the horse and other children took turns on the pony. Several Congressmen and their families attended the exhibit.

In Roseburg, the pencil war continued. "I had no idea what an enormous task we had

Young people from the Washington, D.C. area bring a horse and pony to a busy street in the Georgetown neighborhood to call attention to the plight of the mustangs and to a showing of paintings and sculpture of horses at the Washington Gallery of Art. Gregory Gude, who interested his dad, Congressman Gilbert Gude of Maryland, in introducing the save-the-mustang bill in Congress, sits astride the horse—a sight that stopped traffic on the busy Georgetown thoroughfare.

undertaken," Joan Bolsinger says. "There's nothing simple about getting a law passed. I was up and working from five to seven every morning, five days a week, writing countless letters. There were dozens of phone calls and endless interviews."

Miss Bolsinger even appeared on an Oregon radio show urging people to write to their Congressmen about the mustangs. With her on the program was one of her students, Lynn Williams. "Lynn wrote more letters to more people, did more research, and remembered all the facts better than anyone else," Miss Bolsinger explained.

All the publicity worked. More and more Americans became interested in saving the horses. Sometimes a Congressman has to work hard to "whip up" public interest in a bill he is sponsoring. Not in this case. In one single day, Senator Hatfield reported, he received 25,000 letters about the mustangs!

Congressmen realized that hundreds of thousands of their constituents wanted quick action to make the save-the-horses bills into a good, strong law. So both houses of Congress immediately set dates for committees to hear arguments for and against the bills. The committee hearings were to be held in mid-April.

4
Speaking Up for Mustangs

The huge airplane roared down the runway and rose into the foggy air. Flight 155 from Portland, Oregon, was taking off!

Inside the plane sat two very excited travelers, Joan Bolsinger and Lynn Williams. They were headed for Washington, D.C., to testify in favor of the save-the-horses bills before committees of the House and Senate.

Fastening her seat belt, Joan Bolsinger looked at the boy next to her. "Well, Lynn," she said, "I don't know what we're getting into, but here we go." Solemnly, the two shook hands. As they settled down for the long flight, both were recalling the thrilling events of the past few weeks.

First had come the unexpected invitation

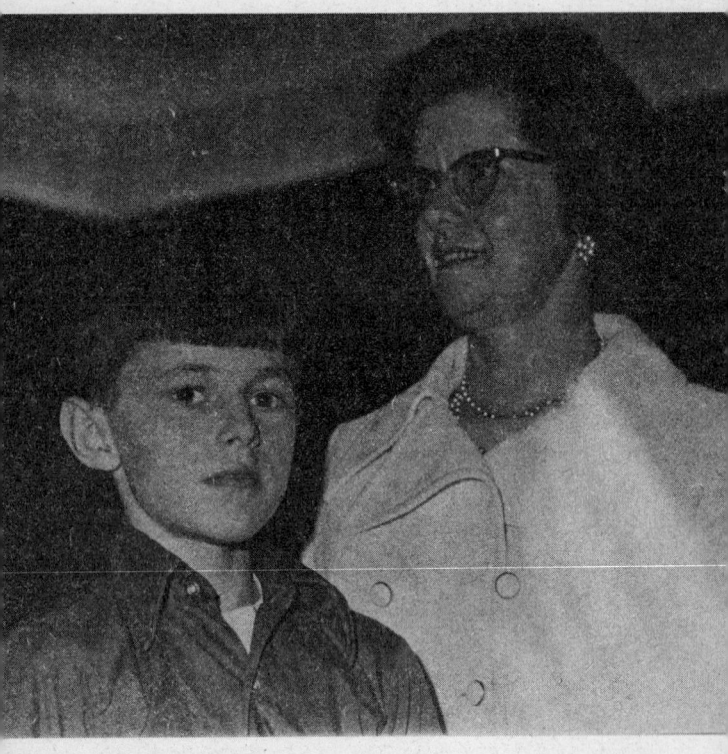

All set for a big trip! Lynn Williams and his teacher, Joan Bolsinger, are about to fly to Washington, D.C. There, they will spend two days testifying before subcommittees of the Senate and the House of Representatives. Lynn and his teacher will tell the subcommittee members why they believe the mustangs should be protected by a strong new law.

Speaking Up for Mustangs

from the American Horse Protection Association. Would Lynn and his teacher like to go to the nation's capital to tell a committee of lawmakers why they believed the mustangs should be protected?

Would they like to go to Washington to help push the bills along their way? Of course they would! But how would they travel the 3,000 miles? Where would they stay? Who would pay for transportation and hotel?

Almost before they had time to worry about these problems, solutions were offered. Pearl Twyne, the president of the American Horse Protection Association, invited Lynn Williams and Joan Bolsinger to stay at her home near Washington. A sixth-grade class in Glen Head, New York, had read about the invitation to Lynn and his teacher. They wanted to help the wild horses, too. So, they offered to pay the two round-trip plane fares. The New York boys and girls raised the necessary money by selling "Save the Mustangs" stickers.

While preparing for the trip, Lynn took time to find out about the Congressional committees that he would be facing. Now, relaxing on the plane, he silently reviewed what he had learned.

As soon as a bill is introduced in either

house of Congress, it is sent to an appropriate committee. A bill to raise the prices farmers can get for their crops might go to the Agricultural Committee. A bill to allow the United States to sell weapons to another country would probably go to the Foreign Relations Committee.

Each bill introduced in the House goes to a House committee. Each bill introduced in the Senate goes to a Senate committee.

Once a bill is *in committee,* the committee members control it. They may hold public hearings on the bill, write a report, and send the bill back to Congress for a vote. Or they may *kill* the bill simply by ignoring it. If a committee—for example, a Senate committee—ignores a bill, the bill's sponsor may send a *discharge petition* to the Senate. If more than half the Senators sign the petition, the committee must hold hearings on the bill. However, a discharge petition seldom gets enough votes.

The House has 21 standing, or permanent, committees. Each committee has about 30 members. New members are chosen from among newly elected Representatives. House Democratic leaders choose which new Democratic Representatives will serve on which committee. Republican leaders do the same

Speaking Up for Mustangs

for new Republicans in the House. A *chairman* heads each committee. The chairman belongs to whichever political party holds the most seats in the House. Committee chairmen are elected in a secret vote by the other members of their party.

Senate committee members are chosen in the same way as in the House. The Senate has 17 standing committees of 7 to 28 members each. Starting in 1977, the Senate will choose committee chairmen just as the House does now.

Lynn knew that he and Miss Bolsinger would be testifying before the Interior Committees of both House and Senate. The Interior Committees work on bills that deal with our natural resources. Like other committees, they are divided into subcommittees. The save-the-horses bills were to go before the Subcommittees on Public Lands, since many mustangs live on these lands.

Sightseeing took up most of Lynn's first day in Washington. On Monday, April 19, he was scheduled to appear before the House Subcommittee on Public Lands.

Lynn and his teacher arrived in Room 1324 of the Longworth House Office Building promptly at nine o'clock in the morning. They blinked at the bright lights and looked curi-

On April 19, Lynn and Miss Bolsinger attended the hearings of the House Subcommittee on Public Lands. Lynn and his teacher (wearing dark glasses) are seated in the front row. Behind them are experts who have studied the needs and habits of wild horses. They are, third from left, Steven Pellegrini; fourth from left, Dr. Michael Pontrelli; and "Wild Horse Annie" Johnston.

ously at the many TV cameras. At 9:45, the subcommittee's chairman, Nevada Representative Walter Baring, called the meeting to order.

"This meeting today," he announced, "has been scheduled for the purpose of taking testimony on legislation designed to authorize protection, management, and control of free-roaming horses and burros on public lands."

Speaking Up for Mustangs

Congressman Baring added that he himself had introduced two save-the-horses bills. He said that he believed the law was needed, but that "as chairman . . . it is my desire to give everyone a chance to be heard. . . . I want to hear all points of view."

Before hearing any testimony, Mr. Baring announced that all the save-the-horses bills would be entered in the official written record of the hearing. He also entered a report on the bills from the Interior Department. The chairman of a committee always requests such a report from the government department that would be responsible for enforcing a new law. The Interior Department's report gave the reactions of department officials to parts of the various bills.

One of the first witnesses to testify was Representative Gude. He described his bill briefly, then grinned at the committee members.

"I have my son with me today," he said, nodding at Greg. "He actually is responsible for my getting involved in this legislation. . . . I would like him to come forward. He has just a few comments about the bill."

"We are happy to have you come before the committee this morning," said Mr. Baring.

"Thank you." Greg leaned forward to speak

into the microphone. "Lots of people have read about the wild mustangs. My Dad and I have gotten about 1,000 letters and petitions supporting the bill. . . . Please approve this bill as soon as possible."

Mr. Baring thanked Greg. "We certainly appreciate your statement," he said.

Representative John Dellenback of Oregon added: "We all realize that what we can contribute as Members of Congress very much depends upon those who give us ideas. We don't dream them all up ourselves. So we are grateful to you for your role in getting this legislation into existence."

Other members of the subcommittee were not so friendly. Opposition to the save-the-horses bills was strong.

One opponent was Representative Wayne Aspinall of Colorado. Mr. Aspinall's constituents included many ranchers who claimed mustangs used up the food their sheep and cattle needed. To please these constituents—who had, after all, helped elect him—Mr. Aspinall planned to work against a strong save-the-horses bill. Several times, he stated that mustangs were just small, ugly animals—not strong, free symbols of the Old West, as Greg and others claimed.

Speaking Up for Mustangs

One of the first witnesses before the House Subcommittee was eleven-year-old Greg Gude. Greg's father had introduced one of the bills being considered by the Subcommittee. Representative Gude sat beside his son, and testified for the bill, too.

"Most of the wild horses are not horses that any of us would look at twice," he told Mr. Gude scornfully. Mr. Aspinall added that ranchers should still be allowed to mix their own horses with the wild bands. This would strengthen the mustangs. "Get some good blood into them," he urged.

SAVE THE MUSTANGS!

Greg and Lynn felt disturbed as they listened to several witnesses agree with this point of view. Allowing ranchers to mix domestic horses with mustangs had been the loophole that permitted mustanging even after the Wild Horse Annie Law was passed.

One witness, Boyd Rasmussen of the Interior Department, suggested that penalties for hunting mustangs should be less than those included in Mr. Gude's bill. He thought a $500 fine and/or six months in jail was enough. On the other hand, a Representative from Pennsylvania said he favored far stiffer penalties—a $10,000 fine and/or ten years in jail.

During the hearing, important facts emerged. The subcommittee learned that although an agency of the Interior Department —the Bureau of Land Management (BLM) —was supposed to protect the mustangs, it was not doing its job. Since 1934, cattlemen and sheepmen had been allowed to graze their animals on the public lands for a small fee. The ranchers claimed that mustangs were eating much of the grass and drinking the water on the public lands. So, instead of protecting the mustangs, the BLM allowed ranchers to kill them.

Subcommittee members began to wonder:

Speaking Up for Mustangs

Should a few ranchers be permitted to destroy life on public lands, just to make more profit for themselves?

One witness, a scientist who had studied the mustangs on the open range, said he was not even sure the mustangs ate the same foods the sheep and cattle did. Certainly, he said, the few mustangs that remained were no threat to ranchers' livestock. His words were backed up by witnesses from the Sierra Club and other conservation groups.

Some testimony surprised Lynn. He listened to another witness say that some ranchers hoped the remaining mustangs would be protected. These ranchers looked on the wild horses as a reminder of the pioneering days of the Old West.

Lynn Williams and Joan Bolsinger did not testify until after five o'clock. Lynn spoke first.

"I am here as a representative of the school children of Oregon. We have been working on this project since the first of January by writing letters to legislators and many other people who might help. We have also been on the radio, TV, and in many newspaper articles."

Then Joan Bolsinger was called. "We wish to submit our plea for passage of this bill for preservation of these last remaining wild

A few months before, only a few people dreamed of trying to save the last beautiful, free-roaming mustangs. But by now, millions of Americans had read about, and come to value highly, these animals that had helped shape their country's history. Many such

Americans waited anxiously as save-the-horses bills began making their way through Congress. The Americans wondered: Would any of the bills lead to a good, new law?

horses—symbols of that freedom and will to survive which all of us in the world today so desperately need."

Unlike the conservationists and scientists who had testified, Lynn and his teacher could not tell the committee about the needs and habits of the mustangs. But they could, and did, tell the Representatives how important the "wild ones" were to thousands of Americans, young and old. Their testimony made it clear that those who loved the mustangs would not give up until a strong protection bill became law.

The Senate Subcommittee hearings were held the next day. This was so that witnesses like Lynn, who had come from far away, would not have to travel to Washington twice.

Again, Lynn and his teacher were on hand early. Senators Jackson and Hatfield, cosponsors of S. 1116, were both members of this Subcommittee. Senator Hatfield told the Subcommittee about the hard work of the two witnesses from Roseburg:

"The fight to save the wild horses has indeed been a children's crusade. I would add it might be called a 'pencil war.' " Senator Hatfield pointed out that, though "it is often difficult for people to translate their concern into positive action," thousands of girls and

"My name is Lynn Williams . . . I am here . . . to testify for S. 1116 to preserve and protect wild horses and burros." Thus Lynn began his statement before the Senate Subcommittee on Public Lands. Miss Bolsinger, sitting next to Lynn, told about her class' concern for the mustangs.

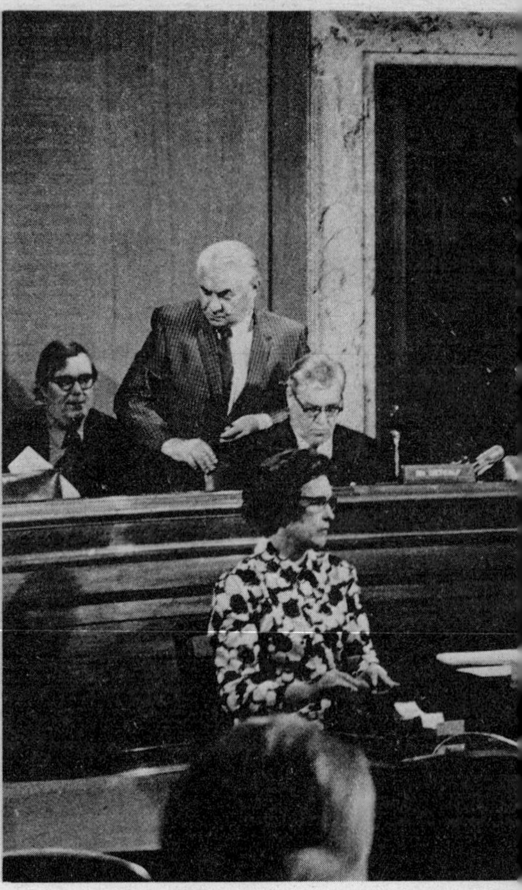

Carefully, the Senators on the Subcommittee listened to the evidence of witnesses. In the center is Senator Church, of Idaho, Chairman of the Subcommittee. On the left is Montana's Senator Metcalf, and Oregon's Senator Hatfield is on the right. In front of the Senators is a reporter who records every word spoken during the hearing. Copies of the entire hearing are printed, and are available to the public. Lynn Williams and Joan Bolsinger are in the front row, their backs to the camera.

boys *had* managed to turn concern into action on behalf of the mustangs.

Lynn and Miss Bolsinger made their statements, and Senator Hatfield asked them a few friendly questions. Then the busy Senator excused himself to attend a meeting of another committee on which he served.

In Room 3110 of the New Senate Office Building, the Senate Subcommittee on Public Lands continued to hear testimony. Most of the witnesses had already testified before the House Subcommittee. Boyd Rasmussen of the Interior Department repeated a suggestion he made to the House subcommittee. "We think we could establish five ranges," he said. People could drive over the ranges in cars to see the mustangs. If the number of horses grew too large for the food supply, government agents would kill some of them without unnecessary cruelty. This way, he explained, there would be enough food for the horses that remained.

Under close questioning, Mr. Rasmussen agreed that the ranges would be expensive: each would cost $3,000,000 to set up and $300,000 each year to maintain after that. Furthermore, the ranges would hold only 3,000 horses altogether, so that hundreds of

Several Subcommittee witnesses presented clear evidence of the cruelties of mustanging. Unknown to mustangers, these witnesses, and people working with them, had photographed captured horses. These mustangs are the dying remains of a herd rounded up in the high mountains of southeastern Idaho.

the mustangs still living would have to be killed off.

Were such ranges needed? A new witness, Dr. Michael Pontrelli, a biologist at the University of Nevada, thought not.

According to Dr. Pontrelli, mustangs should be allowed to share the public lands with many different animals. "I don't like the idea that a preserve will ever be the only place we would find wild horses," he said.

Another witness was Velma Johnston, Wild Horse Annie herself. She made a brief statement and answered questions. The most important part of her testimony was a long report on the past, present, and possible future of the mustangs. Included were photos of horribly wounded horses and newspaper articles about mustangers. There was also evidence that some lawmen were cooperating with mustangers instead of trying to enforce the Wild Horse Annie Law. The report showed that although mustangers had been caught red-handed breaking the law, none had been punished.

Finally, all the witnesses had been heard. Hearings on some bills may last several days. But this hearing took only one day. At 4:45, the tired witnesses left Room 3110. Cameramen packed up their equipment. Reporters dashed off to write their stories.

The Senators leaving the room now knew the facts about the mustangs. They had heard opinions for and against the bills that had been introduced. Their next step would be to consider the testimony and decide whether or not to recommend that the Senate pass a save-the-horses bill. The House Subcommittee on Public Lands faced the same task.

A Congressman's most important duty is to speak up for the people who elected him. He listens to voters' suggestions and opinions, then supports those bills that will benefit the people in his state or district. Here, a Congressman talks with some of his constituents.

5
Two Acts Equal—No Law

By the end of April, Lynn Williams was back at school, telling his classmates about his exciting week in Washington. Together, the fourth graders discussed Congress's next step toward passing a save-the-horses law. The two subcommittees would now decide which bill, if any, to send back to the House and Senate for a vote.

At the same time, in Washington, subcommittee leaders were trying to schedule immediate meetings on the save-the-horses bills. But Congressmen are busy people. They attend Congressional and committee meetings, read letters and reports, meet with constituents, travel, and so on. The earliest date that was convenient for members of the Senate subcommittee to meet was June 16.

This meeting, called an Executive Session, was not open to the public. Carefully, the subcommittee members discussed the testimony they had heard at the public hearing.

One member pointed out to Senator Jackson that his bill called for setting up at least 12 wild horses ranges. Yet several people who had studied mustangs had said that opening special ranges would not be the best way to protect the horses. The mustangs, according to scientists like Dr. Pontrelli, needed the freedom of the open range.

Senator Jackson agreed, and the bill was changed to read that special ranges *might* be set up but not that they *had* to be.

Another Senator remembered that some witnesses had complained that S. 1116 would conflict with laws already in force in some states. These state laws allowed ranchers to round up their own stray horses on public lands.

Sometimes, a new federal law does overturn a state law or laws. For example, a 1964 federal law says that people of all races must be allowed to use such public places as restaurants and swimming pools. This law overturned hundreds of state laws that had

Two Acts Equal—No Law

forbidden blacks to mingle with whites in such places. The federal law was especially planned to overturn the unfair state laws.

However, in the case of the horses, the subcommittee saw no reason to overturn what they believed were fair, needed state laws regarding stray horses. So the Senators changed the definition of a mustang to an "unclaimed," free-roaming horse.

The Executive Session did not take long. The Senators were eager to get a strong save-the-horses law through Congress, and they pretty much agreed on what the law should say. They wrote the changes they thought necessary into the Hatfield-Jackson bill. This is called *marking up*.

Then the subcommittee wrote a report explaining exactly why each change had been made, and sent the rewritten bill and its report to the Senate. The bill and report were printed so every Senator would know exactly what he or she would be voting on. The bill and report were also entered in the Congressional Record, the official written report of each day's activities in Congress.

The Senate vote on S. 1116 came on June 29. Senator Jackson rose to address the members.

"I am certainly pleased that S. 1116 . . . is

Even as Senators and Representatives debated the save-the-horses bills, mustangers continued their brutal work. Men on horseback and carrying a heavy wooden pole prod these captured horses toward the loading chute of a cattle van. Animals that resist will be clubbed and dragged into the truck. The photographer who took this picture and others sent them to Wild Horse Annie. She had them printed in the June 8, 1971, edition of her newsletter.

Two Acts Equal—No Law

to receive such prompt consideration by the full Senate. . . . The need for action is immediate. . . . Hunting and harassment of these animals is happening now at the very time this bill is being considered. . . . I hope that the Senate will demonstrate to the young people of our country the importance, interest, and concern that we have in preserving our wild animals."

Senator Jackson had asked for an immediate vote on the bill because he was sure all or nearly all of the Senators favored it. If the bill had been more controversial, it would have been listed on the Calendar of Bills. This means the vote would have been scheduled for a particular date, and time set aside for the Senate to discuss and debate the bill at length.

After Senator Jackson had finished speaking, one Senator did rise to ask a question. He was a Republican with a sense of humor, and he knew that the symbol of the Democratic Party is a donkey, or burro.

"I note that the bill requires the protection, management, and control of wild, free-roaming horses and burros on public lands," the Senator said. "I should like [to know] whether that includes members of the Democratic Party."

The other Senators laughed.

SAVE THE MUSTANGS!

"Well, there are exceptions to every rule," responded a Democratic Senator, "and we are an exception."

A buzzer rang once, informing Senators that a vote was about to be taken. Committee hearings and other duties keep Congressmen from actually being in Congress all the time it is meeting. The buzzer system—there are several signals, each one meaning something different—tells Congressmen who are elsewhere in the building or in offices when they are needed.

When the Senate President called for a vote, Senator Jackson could see he had been right about the bill's popularity. S. 1116 passed the Senate without a single "nay" vote. It was unanimous!

Not all bills pass so easily. Sometimes debate lasts for days or weeks. Any Senator may offer an amendment to a bill to change it. Each amendment must be debated and voted on separately.

Occasionally, a Senator may *filibuster* to prevent the Senate from voting on a bill at all. A filibustering Senator refuses to *yield the floor*. He simply talks and talks and talks so the Senate does not get a chance to take a vote. When one filibustering Senator tires, another may carry on for him. Eventually,

Once, filibustering was a way a small group of Senators could try to stop a bill they opposed. Some Senators even "camped out" to be on hand to take part in a filibuster or to try to end it. Today, Senate rules have been changed, and a vote by two-thirds of the Senators present can end a filibuster.

SAVE THE MUSTANGS!

the Senators who are not filibustering may become so anxious to adjourn the meeting that they give up trying to get the bill voted upon.

The longest filibuster ever, in 1957, lasted more than 24 hours. Since then, Senate rules have changed. Today, if two-thirds of the Senators present vote to stop a filibuster, the filibustering Senator must yield the floor.

The noncontroversial save-the-horses bill slipped through the Senate easily. No amendments were offered; there was no debate and no filibuster. It passed by a simple voice vote, rather than by a roll-call vote in which each Senator votes "yea" or "nay" aloud as his or her name is called.

Next the bill went to the Secretary of the Senate, who prepared an *engrossed* copy. This copy contained the exact wording and punctuation of the bill as passed by the Senate. Since the Senate had "acted" on the bill by passing it, it was now called an act, rather than a bill. The Engrossed Act was sent to the House of Representatives so the Representatives would know the exact wording of the Senate act.

In the House of Representatives, however, the save-the-horses bills were not moving ahead so smoothly.

At the Executive Session of the House Sub-

Two Acts Equal—No Law

committee on Public Lands, three Representatives—Aspinall of Colorado, Dingell of Michigan, and Melchor of Montana—insisted on adding amendments to weaken the bills. One amendment gave state wildlife agencies a strong voice in managing the mustangs. Yet these were some of the same agencies that had cooperated with mustangers over the years!

Another amendment said mustangs could be "removed" from the public lands by "normal" means. But what did this mean? It was "normal" for most mustangers to work in a cruel and brutal way. "Normally," they crippled horses with buckshot and drove them, bleeding, thirsty, and hungry, to slaughterhouses. If the new law allowed "normal" removal of mustangs, it would allow the very same thing it was supposed to stop!

In yet another change, the subcommittee dropped the section of the Gude bill that outlawed releasing domestic horses into the wild bands.

Several members of the subcommittee fought such changes, but they were unsuccessful. The bill reported back to the House included the controversial amendments. Since the "markup" had changed the original bills so much, the new bill was given a new number—H.R. 9098. It was much weaker than the act that had passed in the Senate.

Marking up the House bill took so long that it was not until fall that H.R. 9098 was reported back to the House. That any bill at all, even a weak one, was reported was due largely to subcommittee member John Dellenback. Mr. Dellenback was an Oregon Representative from the district that includes Roseburg.

In September, Lynn Williams (now a fifth grader) and his classmates wrote to Mr. Dellenback urging him to try to get a save-the-horses bill out of committee. Joan Bolsinger's new fourth graders wrote to Mr. Dellenback, too.

Back in the House, H.R. 9098 went before the powerful House Rules Committee.

Before a bill may be debated and voted on in the House, it must receive a *rule* from the Rules Committee. This rule tells how much time will be allowed to debate the bill, how amendments may be made, and so forth. If most Rules Committee members oppose a particular bill, they can refuse to give it a rule. This means the House cannot debate and vote on the bill at all. Only a vote by two-thirds of the House members can force a bill out of an unfriendly Rules Committee.

H.R. 9098 met no opposition from the

Two Acts Equal—No Law

Rules Committee. In fact, the bill was so weak and noncontroversial that it was placed on the *Consent Calendar,* which meant it would be passed without any discussion. A more controversial bill would have been put on the *Union Calendar* (if it called for spending money) or on the *House Calendar* (if it did not call for spending money).

The House vote was set for October 4, 1971. Early in the afternoon, the clerk *called the bill,* which announced that it was up for consideration. Unless a Representative objected, the bill would automatically be passed.

"Is there any objection?" the Speaker asked.

Representative Gude thought some time should be allowed for debating the bill.

"I do object," he said. After a brief exchange between Mr. Gude and the Speaker, it was decided to drop H.R. 9098 for the moment and bring it up later, when there would be more time for discussion.

Later in the day, the Speaker recognized Representative Walter Baring, who said, "I move to suspend the rules and pass H.R. 9098."

The Clerk read the bill section by section. This is called the *Second Reading,* although it

Even while the Senate and the House of Representatives are actually meeting, a Congressman's many duties may keep him busy in his office, or in other parts of the Capitol. These Congressmen are holding an informal discussion—perhaps about a bill that will soon be acted upon. When a vote is about to be taken, a buzzer will sound, recalling the legislators to the House or Senate floor.

is the only time the entire bill is read aloud in the House.

After the reading, Congressman Aspinall spoke. "Mr. Speaker, I rise in support of H.R. 9098...." He explained the changes the subcommittee had made in the original bills.

Other Representatives offered opinions.

Two Acts Equal—No Law

Congressman Saylor of Arizona said, "I rise in mild support of H.R. 9098. . . . I recognize it as the best bill we could get out of the Committee. . . . Personally, I would prefer a much stronger bill."

Mr. Gude said he was pleased by the new bill, even though the section against releasing domestic horses into wild bands had been dropped. He said he had come to believe that wild horse bands sometimes needed the "new blood" of domestic horses. Besides, he added, he felt that the bill as a whole was stronger than the Wild Horse Annie Law—strong enough to protect the mustangs.

About a dozen Representatives spoke in favor of the bill. One, John Davis of Georgia, displayed 86 letters he had received from girls and boys who wanted to save the horses.

It was time to vote. A buzzer sounded, and the bill received its *Third Reading*—by title only. It was passed unanimously. The Engrossed Act was prepared and sent to the Senate. At the same time, the House returned the Senate's Engrossed Act.

Save-the-horses acts had been passed in both the House and the Senate. But there was still no *law*. Until—and unless—House and Senate passed identical acts, the mustang slaughter would continue!

At a Conference Committee meeting, Senators and Representatives try to work out differences in Acts passed by each house of Congress. There were eight major points of difference between the save-the-horses Acts passed by the House and Senate. On most of these points, the Conference Committee members agreed to use the stronger wording of the Senate Act.

6

A Law at Last

"What'll happen now?" Greg Gude asked his father sadly the day after the House passed its save-the-horses act. "Horses are being killed right now, you know."

"I know, Greg. I imagine the Senate will work fast. Since they have the two different Engrossed Acts, it's up to them to ask for a *Conference Committee*. The committee will iron out differences in two acts. Then the House and Senate will agree on a compromise."

"I hope so," Greg responded gloomily.

Mr. Gude turned out to be right. Nine days later, the House act was presented to the Senate.

After the reading, West Virginia Senator

Byrd spoke: "I move that the Senate disagree to the amendments of the House of Representatives and request a conference."

Five Senators, including Mark Hatfield, were named to serve on the Conference Committee. A formal request for the Conference was sent to the House. In the House, Mr. Aspinall asked his fellow Representatives to agree to the Conference. They did agree, without any objection, and five Representatives were named to the Committee.

The Conference Committee met on November 11. This meeting, like all Conference Committee meetings, was closed to the public.

The members moved quickly. Senators and Representatives agreed that there were eight main points of difference between the Senate act and the House act. The committee members worked out these differences. Most of the time, they chose the stronger language of the Senate act over the weaker House act.

In the final version, for instance, the state wildlife agencies were given only a small role in managing the mustangs. Even more important, the section that would permit mustangs to be removed by "normal" means was taken out altogether. Penalties for breaking the law were set at a $2,000 fine and/or a year in prison.

A Law at Last

At the end of only an hour, the Conference Committee had completed its work—and faced a new problem. To make the new wording official, the committee had to vote to accept it. And to vote, the committee needed a *quorum*—the presence of at least five of its ten members. Only four members had actually come to the meeting. The other six were busy elsewhere.

"Well, I know where Hatfield is, at least," said one committee member. "He's home sick in bed. Let's rout him out, get him over here, and take the vote!"

A message was sent to Senator Hatfield's home, and late in the afternoon, the pale, tired Senator appeared. Quickly, the Conference Committee voted to accept the final version of the act. Yet another report was written, this one to explain the differences between the House act and the Senate act, and to tell how these differences had been worked out. If several committee members had disagreed with the final wording, they would have written their own report, as well.

The rewritten act and its report went back to the House. On December 2, Representative Baring asked to be recognized.

"Mr. Speaker, I call up the conference report on the bill to require the protection, management, and control of wild, free-roaming horses and burros on public lands."

Baring explained the actions of the committee—he, too, had been a member—and spoke in favor of the bill. Several other Representatives joined him.

The favorable report by the Conference Committee convinced most House members to support the compromise bill. No one spoke against it. Mr. Baring suggested that members of the House be given five working days to raise objections to the wording of the act. If no one did object to it, the report would be officially accepted and the rewritten bill would pass.

At the end of five days, no objections had been raised. A strong save-the-horses act had cleared the House!

Senate action was rapid, too. The Conference report was presented there on December 3, and no one objected to it. The Secretary of the Senate prepared an *enrolled* copy of the act. This copy contained the precise wording of the act as agreed upon by House and Senate. When it was ready, the enrolled copy was checked over very carefully by a special committee. Finally, a slip, which stated that the enrolled copy was absolutely correct in every detail, was attached.

A Law at Last

On December 6, the Speaker of the House of Representatives signed the enrolled act, and the President of the Senate signed it the next day. On December 8, the signed act was delivered to President Richard Nixon.

Now began a new period of anxious waiting for those who had worked so hard to save the mustangs. The President had ten days in which to act. During that time, he could sign the act and make it a United States law. He could veto the act—refuse to sign it and send it back to Congress with a statement saying why he would not sign it.

Or the President could decide to do neither. If he did not act for ten days *during which Congress was meeting,* the act would become law without his signature. If he took no action, for ten days, *and Congress adjourned during that time,* the act would automatically be vetoed. This is called a *pocket veto*. The process received its nickname because Presidents were said simply to put bills in their pockets.

What if the President vetoed the save-the-horses act? Might it never become law, even though both houses of Congress had passed it?

The answer is: it still could become law. A regular veto, in which the President returns an unsigned act to Congress, may be overturned. If two-thirds of the members of the Senate and two-thirds of the members of the House of Representatives vote in favor of a vetoed act, the act becomes law. Congress does not overturn many vetoes, but it does do so sometimes. A pocket veto, however, cannot be overturned, since Congress would not be meeting at the time of the veto.

The veto system has a purpose. It allows Congress and the President to share the power to make laws. For example, the President may want a certain change in a bill Congress is debating. He announces that he will veto the act unless Congress makes the change he wants. Congress may agree to the change and give the President *his* way. But if enough Congressmen are strongly opposed to the change, they will write the bill the way they want it. Then they will try to overturn the President's veto and get *their* way.

The voice of the public is heard in this part of the lawmaking process, too. After the save-the-horses act reached President Nixon, letters began reaching him, too. These letters urged him to sign the act quickly. Newspaper articles pointed out that, even now, mustang roundups were going on. Editorials urged Nixon to sign the act at once.

A Law at Last

The days dragged slowly for the thousands of Americans who had worked for the mustangs. "Every time the phone rings," said Wild Horse Annie Johnston, "I think it's someone calling to say the President has signed."

On December 17, nine days after Nixon had received the act from Congress, that call did come to Mrs. Johnston's Nevada home. The President had signed the act!

The last step in passing a Federal law—the signing of the final act by the President of the United States. Often the signing ceremony is attended by high government officials.

85 STAT.] PUBLIC LAW 92-195–DEC. 15, 1971 649

Public Law 92-195

AN ACT

December 15, 1971
[S. 1116]

To require the protection, management, and control of wild free-roaming horses and burros on public lands.

Wild horses and burros.
Protection.

Be it enacted by the Senate and House of Representatives of the United States of America in Congress assembled, That Congress finds and declares that wild free-roaming horses and burros are living symbols of the historic and pioneer spirit of the West; that they contribute to the diversity of life forms within the Nation and enrich the lives of the American people; and that these horses and burros are fast disappearing from the American scene. It is the policy of Congress that wild free-roaming horses and burros shall be protected from capture, branding, harassment, or death; and to accomplish this they are to be considered in the area where presently found, as an integral part of the natural system of the public lands.

SEC. 2. As used in this Act—

Definitions.

(a) "Secretary" means the Secretary of the Interior when used in connection with public lands administered by him through the Bureau of Land Management and the Secretary of Agriculture

Copies of all new laws are printed so they will be available to anyone who wants to read or study them. New laws are also added to the Statutes at Large and to the United States Code.

A Law at Last

Just a year before, protecting the mustangs had been a dream. Now it was a law—P.L. 92-195: the 195th public law passed by the Ninety-Second Congress.

As soon as the law was signed, it was printed so a copy would be available to any citizen who wanted to study it. The law was also added to the *Statutes at Large*. This is a collection of volumes containing all laws passed by Congress in the order in which they are passed.

Finally, P.L. 92-195 was entered in the *United States Code*. The Code contains all permanent federal laws, arranged according to subject. The new law took its place in the Code with the Wild Horse Annie Law. Any future mustang law will go in the same part of the Code.

When Joan Bolsinger heard of the signing, she printed the good news in huge letters on the blackboards in her own fourth grade and in Lynn Williams' fifth-grade room. The students cheered.

"No one could give me a Christmas present to top that!" she told them.

Before long, the Roseburg students had new reason to cheer. Senator Mark Hatfield planned to visit their school to thank them for their part in passing the new law.

Soon after P.L. 92–195 became law, Senator Mark Hatfield visited Roseburg, Oregon. He thanked the Roseburg students for all they had done to help save the mustangs. Finally, he presented a pen, used in signing the law, to Lynn who gave it to his school. You can see Lynn's head behind the Senator.

A Law at Last

Large signs greeted the Senator as he entered the school library: WELCOME, SENATOR HATFIELD. THANK YOU, SENATOR.

"This is a real victory for you," Senator Hatfield told the gathered students and teachers. He praised the students for their willingness to take an active part in the government of their country. "Even though you can't yet vote, you have the right to make recommendations to the government," he pointed out.

Then Hatfield asked Lynn Williams to step forward. "I was never so proud to be an Oregonian as I was the day Lynn Williams testified," he said. He gave Lynn one of the pens President Nixon had used to sign the Act into law. Later, Lynn asked to have the pen put on permanent display in the school library.

Roseburg was not the only scene of rejoicing. All across the country, everyone who had ever written a letter or signed a petition on behalf of the horses shared in the feeling that he or she had played a part in the making of a law. The Glen Head, New York, students who had raised money for Lynn Williams' trip to Washington knew their work had paid off. In Maryland, Greg Gude received the congratulations of his father, and he also received another of the pens Nixon had used in signing the law. (Presidents often use several pens for signing so they can give souvenir pens to various people.)

Which of the rejoicing Americans was *most* responsible for the new law? The president of the American Horse Protection Association praised the work of Congress. "Had there not been forceful Congressmen willing to manage a strong bill through Congress," Mrs. Twyne said, "the children's efforts would have been to no avail."

Senator Jackson disagreed. He believed the public—especially boys and girls—were responsible for getting the law. "They made it happen," he wrote.

Joan Bolsinger summed it up. " 'We the people' passed that law. We *are* the people— you, Lynn Williams, I, *all* of us who must make our government work as it was intended, for *all*."

And then she added, "Now comes the really hard part—making the law work."

7
Making It Work

Joan Bolsinger was right. Passing a law is only a beginning. Unless people know that the law will be strictly enforced, they will not obey it. How can we make sure P.L. 92-195 will work?

One way is by seeing that the government punishes anyone who breaks the law. A suspected mustanger may be brought into court and put on trial. If he is found guilty, he may be punished according to the penalties set forth in P.L. 92-195.

Many private citizens are helping the government guard against mustanging. Late in 1971, Wild Horse Annie founded a group called Wild Horse Organized Assistance (WHOA). WHOA sends volunteer patrols

Today, a group called Wild Horse Organized Assistance (WHOA) helps enforce P.L. 92–195. WHOA, founded by Wild Horse Annie, watches for, and reports on, illegal mustanging. Members also help guard the wild ones against natural disasters such as extreme cold or fierce storms. Here, a high school student who is a member of WHOA comforts a wild colt found starving on a wintry Wyoming range.

Making It Work

into the remote areas where mustangs roam. If patrol members find signs of illegal mustanging—as they have several times since 1971—they report it to the Bureau of Land Management. If the BLM is slow to act against the mustangers, a newsletter informs WHOA members about the situation. The newsletter urges everyone who cares about the wild ones to write to the BLM or to their Congressmen to demand vigorous enforcement of P.L. 92-195. And attempts to change the law to allow more mustanging are also being fought by WHOA.

Today, P.L. 92-195 is the law of the land. It stands like a shield between the roaming mustangs and their would-be killers. People built that shield. And only people can make it work.

Glossary

Act The name given to a bill after it has been "acted upon"—passed—by the Senate or the House of Representatives.

Amendment An addition to a bill.

Bill Proposal for a law introduced in a law-making body, such as Congress.

Bureau of Land Management United States government agency in charge of caring for our public lands.

Calendar List of bills in the order in which they will be discussed and voted upon. Three House of Representatives calendars are: the *Union Calendar* (for bills which require spending public money); the *House Calendar* (for bills not requiring such spending); and the *Consent Calendar* (for non-controversial bills). In the Senate, bills are placed on the *Calendar of Bills*.

GLOSSARY

Clerk of the House Official of the House of Representatives elected by his fellow members.

Committee Small group of Senators or Representatives who listen to arguments for and against bills having to do with a particular subject. After hearing testimony, the committee sends a report—with its reasons for supporting or opposing the bill—back to the Senate or the House.

Conference Committee Group made up of both Senators and Representatives. The Committee meets if different forms of the same bill have been passed by both the House and Senate. Committee members try to iron out the differences between the two bills.

Congressional Record Complete report of each meeting of the Senate and the House of Representatives.

Constituents People who have elected a particular man or woman to office.

Discharge petition Formal request by Congressmen for a committee to hold hearings on a bill, when the committee has been delaying such action.

Engrossed Act Copy of an act exactly as it has been passed by *either* the House or the Senate.

Enrolled Act Copy of an act exactly as it has been passed by *both* the House and the Senate.

Executive Session Congressional committee meeting to which the public is not invited.

First Reading Action of the Clerk of the House in giving each bill a number as it is introduced.

GLOSSARY

Filibuster Method of delaying action on a bill in the Senate. Today, a filibuster—a series of long speeches by Senators opposing a bill—may be ended by a vote of two-thirds of the Senators present.

Interior Department That part of the United States government in charge of the use and protection of the land, its natural resources, and so forth.

Lobbyist Someone paid by a group or organization to try to persuade Congressmen to vote in favor of bills which will help that group.

Mark-up Form of a bill reported back to Congress by a committee. The mark-up contains the committee's suggestions for changes in the original bill.

President of the Senate Vice-president of the United States, one of whose duties it is to run Senate meetings. When he is too busy to do so, his place is taken by a "temporary president," elected by his fellow Senators.

Quorum The number of members of a group needed to be present in order for the group to carry on business.

Roll call vote Each Congressman votes when his name is called aloud.

Rules Committee House committee that decides when bills may be voted on, how long debate will be, and so on.

GLOSSARY

Second Reading Reading of a complete bill in the House of Representatives just before the bill is debated.

Speaker of the House Highest official of the House of Representatives, elected by his fellow members to run meetings.

Statutes at Large Collection of all United States laws in the order in which they were passed.

Subcommittee Division of a Congressional committee. Each subcommittee is concerned with just one area of the matters that the entire committee deals with.

Third Reading Reading of a bill's title only, just before members of the House vote upon it.

United States Code Collection of all United States laws arranged according to the subject matter of the laws.

Veto Action of a United States President in refusing to sign an Act passed by Congress—and thus preventing it from becoming law. A vote by two-thirds of the members of each house of Congress can overturn a veto. A *pocket veto* occurs when a President refuses to sign an Act when Congress is not meeting—so that Congress has no chance to overturn the veto.

Index

A
act, 66-79
Agricultural Committee, 40
amendments, 64, 66-67, 74
American Horse Protection Association, 34, 39, 84
animal range. *See* mustangs
Arizona, 70
Aspinall, Wayne, Representative, 44-45, 67, 69-70, 74

B
Baring, Walter, Representative, 42-44, 69, 75-76
Bethesda, Maryland, 13
bill, 7, 19, 22-72; calling the, 69; engrossed copy of, 66, 71; introduction of, 28-32; killing of, 40
Bill Clerk, 29
Bolsinger, Joan, 2, 4, 6, 7-9, 11, 34, 36, 37-41, 47, 50-54, 68, 79, 81, 84, 85
Bureau of Land Management (BLM), 46, 87
burros, wild, 22, 25, 31. *See also* mustangs
Byrd, Senator, 73-74

C
Calendar of Bills, 63
cattle, 6, 44, 46, 47
children's crusade, 50
Clerk of the House, 29, 69
Colorado, 44, 67
Conference Committee, 73-76
Congress, U.S., 7-17, 29-30; buzzer system of, 64, 71; committees, 37, 39; committee hearings, 36, 39-54, 54-56; session of, 12-13; subcommittees, 41-57
Congressional Record, 61
Congressman. *See* Congress, U.S.
Congresswomen. *See* Congress, U.S.
Consent Calendar, 69
constituents, 19, 36, 44, 58, 59

D
Davis, Representative, 71
Dellenback, John, Representative, 44, 68

INDEX

Democratic party, 29-30, 40, 63
Dingell, Representative, 67
discharge petition, 40
district, Congressional, 9, 15, 19

E
Engrossed Act, 66, 71
Enrolled Act, 76-77
Eugene, Oregon, 9
Executive Sessions, 60-61, 66-67

F
feral, 22, 25
filibuster, 64-66
First Reading, 28-29
Foreign Relations Committee, 40

G
Georgia, 71
Glen Head, New York, 39, 83
Government Printing Office, 29
Gude, Gilbert, Representative, 13, 15-17, 19, 22-23, 25-28, 32, 33-34, 43-46, 67, 69, 71, 73
Gude, Gregory, 13, 15-17, 19, 22, 25, 28, 32, 34, 43-46, 73, 83

H
Hatfield, Mark, Senator, 9, 11, 29-32, 36, 50, 52-53, 54, 74-75, 81, 83
hopper, 28-29
House Calendar, 69

H.R. 795, 29. *See also* H.R. 9098
H.R. 9098, 68-71

I
in committee, 40
Indians, American, 4
Interior Committees, 41
Interior, U.S. Department of, 46, 54

J
Jackson, Henry, Senator, 29-32, 50, 60-61, 63-64, 84
Johnston, Velma "Wild Horse Annie," 13-15, 56, 79, 85-87

L
law, federal, 6, 8, 77-79, 80-81, 82, 84, 87; enforcing of, 87-89; penalties for breaking, 87; repeal of, 23
lawmakers, 6, 7-8, 32, 39. *See also* Congress, U.S.
lawyer, 23, 25
Lewis and Clark Expedition, 4
lobbyist, 16-17
Longworth House Office Building, 41
loophole, 15, 23, 46

M
McCune, Steve, 11
marking-up, 61, 67-68
Maryland, 13, 83
Melchor, Representative, 67
Michigan, 67
Montana, 67

INDEX

mustangers, 2, 11, 23, 56, 67
mustangs, description of, 1; history of, 2, 4; illegal hunting of, 1-3, 4, 6, 11-12, 15, 56, 67; mixing of, 15, 45-46, 71; penalties for hunting, 23, 25, 46, 74; population of, 4; protection of, 7, 11, 22, 42, 87-89; ranges, 23, 25, 54, 56, 60

N
National Geographic, 12
Nevada, 42, 79
New Senate Office Building, 54
New World, the, 2
Nixon, Richard M., 77, 79, 83. *See also* President, U.S.

O
Oregon, 2, 4, 9, 11, 29, 44, 47, 68

P
pencil war, 6, 9-10, 32, 34, 50
Pennsylvania, 46
petition, 32-34, 44
P.L. 92-195, 81, 85, 87. *See also* H.R. 795, H.R. 9098, S. 1116
pocket veto, 77-78
Pontrelli, Dr. Michael, 56, 60
Pony Express, 4

Portland, Oregon, 37
President, U.S., signing of act by, 77-79, 80-81; pens used by, 83, 84
public lands, 23, 25, 41, 42, 46-47, 54, 56, 60, 66-67
publicity, 32, 36

Q
quorum, 75

R
ranchers, 6, 15, 44-47
Rasmussen, Boyd, 46, 54
Reno, Nevada, 13
Representatives, House of, 8-9, 13, 25, 26-27, 28; committees, 40-41; subcommittee meetings, 41-57, 66-67. *See also* Congress, U.S.
Republican party, 29-30, 40-41
roll call vote, 66
Roseburg, Oregon, 2, 6, 9, 34, 50, 68, 82, 83
rule, 68
Rules Committee, 68

S
S. 1116, 32, 50, 60-61, 63-64
save-the-mustangs legislation. *See* H.R. 795, H.R. 9098, S. 1116
Saylor, Representative, 70-71
Second Reading, 69
Senate, U.S., 8-9, 28-31; committees of, 40-41; Secretary of, 66; subcommittees, 50-57, 60-61;

INDEX

Senate, U.S., (*Cont.*)
    temporary president of, 28; voice vote, 66. *See also* Congress, U.S.
sheep, 6, 44, 46, 47
Sierra Club, 47
Spanish explorers, 2, 4
Speaker of the House, 28, 69-70, 75-76, 77
Statutes at Large, 81

T
Third Reading, 71
Twyne, Pearl, 39, 84

U
Union Calendar, 69
United States Code, 81
University of Nevada, 56

V
veto, 77-78
Vice-President, U.S., 28

W
Washington, D.C., 6, 7, 16, 37-39, 41, 59, 85
Washington *Star*, 34
Washington State, 29
West Virginia, 73-74
Wild Horse Annie Law, 13-15, 23, 46, 56, 71, 81
Wild Horse Organized Assistance (WHOA), 85-87
wild ones. *See* mustangs
Williams, Lynn, 36, 37-39, 41-42, 46, 47, 50-54, 59, 68, 81, 82, 83

Y
yield the floor, 64, 66

POCKET BOOKS

ARCHWAY
PAPERBACKS

Other titles you will enjoy

29770 PERPLEXING PUZZLES AND TANTALIZING TEASERS, by Martin Gardner. Illustrated by Laszlo Kubinyi. A fascinating collection of puzzles and teasers to challenge your wits, tickle your funny bone, and give you and your friends hours of entertainment. (95¢)

29644 SEA MONSTERS, written and illustrated by Walter Buehr. A fascinating discussion of the myths, facts, and scientific theories about the existence of giant sea creatures from prehistoric times to the present. (75¢)

29524 DON'T TAKE TEDDY, by Babbis Friis-Baastad. Translated from the Norwegian by Lise Sømme McKinnon. Mikkel doesn't want his older retarded brother put away in an institution, so he escapes with him on a desperate journey across the countryside. (75¢)

29511 FLY-BY-NIGHT, written and illustrated by K. M. Peyton. Ruth faces the challenge of training her spirited pony while learning to ride herself—and finds it a tough, exciting, and sometimes terrifying experience. (75¢)

29726 THE HAPPY DOLPHINS, by Samuel Carter III. Illustrated with photographs. The author explores many intriguing facets of dolphin behavior as he tells the true story of Dal and Suwa, two bottle-nosed dolphins who made friends with humans. ($1.25)

29746 KIDS COOKING: *A First Cookbook for Children,* by Aileen Paul and Arthur Hawkins. Easy to prepare recipes for desserts, party foods, snacks, breakfast, lunch, and dinner dishes are included in this basic guide to the fun of cooking for girls and boys. ($1.25)

29739 THE BOY'S BOOK OF BIKING, by Allan A. Macfarlan. Illustrated by Paulette Macfarlan. This expert handbook gives detailed information on how to buy a bike, ride like a pro, play games of skill, stay safe on wheels, make repairs, plan trips, and form clubs. ($1.25)

29634 MARTIN LUTHER KING: *The Peaceful Warrior,* by Ed Clayton. Illustrated by David Hodges. The moving story of Dr. King's childhood in Atlanta, his career as one of the greatest black leaders of our time, and his tragic assassination. (75¢)

(If your bookseller does not have the titles you want, you may order them by sending the retail price, plus 25¢ (50¢ if you order two or more books) for postage and handling to: Mail Service Department, POCKET BOOKS, a division of Simon & Schuster, Inc., 1 West 39th Street, New York, N. Y. 10018. Please enclose check or money order—do not send cash.)